Teach a friend to read and write

**If you can read
you can teach reading and writing**

**Just read the short and simple instructions
and then start teaching a friend, family member
or neighbour of any age to read and write.**

Dyslexia-friendly

ACKNOWLEDGEMENTS

The Teach A Friend To Read And Write Campaign would like to
thank the following for their help in producing
TEACH AND WRITE A FRIEND TO READ AND WRITE

Miriam Mason-Sesay MBE, Country Director of Educaid S.L.
Linda Curtis, Moon Englefield, Una Sadler and Anne West of We CAN Read
Robert Littleford, Hand Drawn World
Father Martin Morgan, St Margaret Church Rottingdean
Graham Rankin, Documentary Maker, Hemsworth Reflections
His Excellency Eddie M.Turay, Ambassador to Sierra Leone
The People's Book Prize Literacy Campaigners

Published by Delancey Press Ltd
23 Berkeley Square
London W1J 6HE
www.delanceypress.co.uk

Copyright © M.E.L.G. Tate 2015
The right of M.E.L.G. Tate to be identified as the author of this work has been asserted by him in accordance with the Copyright Design and Patents Acts of 1988. All rights reserved under International Copyright Conventions. No part of this publication may be reproduced, stored or transmitted in any form or by any means without prior permission in writing from the publisher. Reviewers may quote brief passages.

First published 2015
Front cover photograph by Italiaander: www.italiaander.co.uk
Phonic Alphabet Poster by Robert Littleford: Hand Drawn World
Printed and bound in the UK by 4 Edge Ltd.
A CIP catalogue record for this title is available from the British Library

ISBN 978-1-907205-30-9

Ben (18) tells us:

The instructions are really simple and short — you just read through them and then start coaching.

First I taught my little sister to read and write. She is seven and has dyslexia, like me. Now she is doing well at school, and she is using computers and texting all her friends.

My new reader from next door is 66, and learning to read totally changed her life. Now she goes on buses and trains and to the shops on her own. She reads the labels on her medicine bottles and doctor's prescriptions.
She loves being able to read recipes, magazines, letters and texts and she gets a big kick from filling in forms by herself. She has just started IT classes.

And my older sister is teaching her best mate, who is 24, so that she will be able to teach her children to read and write.

Send in your stories and photos to :
www.teachafriendtoread.com
and inspire everyone to teach a friend
to read and write.

Dear Reading Coach

Repetition, encouragement and fun through paired reading
are the keys to learning to read.
Please read to each other for 20 minutes or more every day.

**It is very important to begin at the beginning
and cover every bit of *Teach a friend to read and write*,
even if your new reader can already read a little.**

Teaching letter-sounds (phonics)

Start off by teaching the letter-sounds, using the alphabet poster, pointing out the same-shape pictures :
apple, brush, cat, duck, elephant, etc.

When naming the letters, use ONLY letter-sounds (phonics)
So don't say the alphabet names: ay, bee, cee, dee, ee, ef, gee, aitch, eye, jay....

To make sure that you always pronounce the phonic reading letters correctly, practise on your own before you start with your learner.
To get the right sound pretend to stutter :
eg **a** (as you say it in abracadabra) apple **a...a...a...a**(pple),
brush **b...b...b...b**(rush), cat **c...c...c...c**(at)

When you teach the phonic reading letters to your learner, they will pronounce the letter-sound only once.
eg. Coach: *What is that picture?* New reader: *It is a brush.*
    Coach : *What is that letter?*   New reader: *It is **b** like brush*

The exception letter **x** is pronounced kiss, said quickly (**ks**).
Call the letter-sound **c** the curly **c**; and **k** the kicking **k.**
Explain that the letter-sound **q** is followed by a silent **u (qu).**

Teach the large letter-sounds only after your new reader is totally confident with all small letters, after page ten.

Artwork by Robert Littleford, *Hand Drawn World*

To teach 3-letter words:
slide each letter-sound into the next:

| c...a...n = can | h...e...n = hen | s...i...x = six | d...o...g = dog |
| b...u...g = bug | f...a...t = fat | j...e...t = jet | k...i...t – kit |

Problem letters and words:
If your new reader misreads a word or hesitates,
wait four seconds or more....
and then you say the word correctly in a calm neutral voice.
Underline your reader's problem letter-sound or word and practise it later.

'Say as you copy' :

Ask your new reader to copy their problem letter or word from the book, five times or more, saying the letter-sound or word as they are writing it.

This imprints the shape of the letter or whole word in the new reader's brain.

Repetition:
Repeat each exercise or reading page until your new reader is confident.

Praise Boxes:
Enter your new reader's name in the praise box at the end of each page when your new reader can read the whole page to you without a misread.

Writing
Use the writing practice pages at the back only after your new reader recognises all small and all large letters correctly and with confidence.

Coco the chimp's story practises all the essential basic reading skills through repetition.
Read the whole of the new page you are working on out loud to your new reader first. This will give your new reader confidence.
Then your new reader can read the page back to you again and again, as often as necessary.

Punctuation: Full-stop, Comma and Question mark:

a full-stop: Your new reader should always stop and pause for one or two seconds.
a comma: Your new reader should pause for a second.
a question mark: Explain this shows that a question has been asked.

Some tips for dealing with your new reader's difficult letters :

Make the shape of the letter with your hands or your body.
Sing the letter to a well-known tune instead of using the words.
Write the problem letter on paper, or in the earth or sand.
Call the problem letter your 'special letter' and say for instance,
*Quick, quick, let's practise reading our special letter **q** quickly.*
Point at the letter and ask your new reader to whisper its letter-sound,
and then to say it louder and louder.

Does your new reader need an eye test or a hearing test?

If your new reader appears to have difficulty seeing the letters clearly – perhaps peering or holding the book closer or further away – you should help to arrange an eye test.

If your new reader has difficulty hearing or repeating some of the letter-sounds you make, you should help to arrange a hearing test.

**Please remember to use *Say as you copy*
for your new reader's problem letters and words
throughout the reading adventure.**

You are now ready to start teaching your learner to read:

Point at each image and make sure that your learner knows what each object is, and has imprinted it in their mind.

eg. Coach: *What is that picture?* New reader: *It is a brush.*

　　Coach: *What is that picture?* New reader*: It is a worm.*

Then point at each letter:

(When you teach the letter-sounds to your learner, they will pronounce the letter-sound only once.)

eg. Coach: *What is that letter?* New reader: *It is **f** like fish.*

　　Coach: *What is that letter?* New reader: *It is **d** like duck.*

The exception letter **x** is pronounced kiss, said quickly (**ks**).

Call the letter-sound **c** the curly **c**; and **k** the kicking **k**.

Explain that the letter-sound **q** is followed by a silent **u (qu)**.

Coach point under each small letter and new reader read.
Coach tick correct letters.
Coach underline problem letters and practise them later.
If your new reader hesitates or says a letter-sound incorrectly,
wait 4 seconds....Then you say the letter-sound correctly. (Not ay bee cee dee !)

tick	day 1 ✓	day 2 ✓		tick	day 1 ✓	day 2 ✓
s				v		
a				l		
t				o		
i				z		
p				j		
n				u		
c				w		
k				y		
e				f		
h				b		
q				r		
m				d		
g				x		

x   x   x...

Coach : show your new reader how to blend, using the word cat.

Point under **c** and say it...slide to **a** and say it...slide to **t** and say it.
Then say whole word **cat.**
Ask your new reader to copy you, saying   **c...a...t   cat.**
Then ask your reader to try the rest of the words for themselves.
If your reader hesitates or says a word incorrectly,
wait 4 seconds....Then <u>you</u> say the word correctly.

c...a...t   cat

r...a...t   rat

h...a...t   hat

v...a...n   van

m...a...n   man

b...a...t   bat

h...e...n   hen

hot..

m...e...n   men

l...e...g   leg

j...e...t   jet

w...e...b   web

s...u...n   sun

n...u...t   nut

g...u...n   gun

p...i...g   pig

z...i...p   zip

hot hot hot..

k...i...d   kid

f...o...x   fox

l...o...g   log

d...o...g   dog

b...o...x   box

b...u...g   bug

a...n...t   ant

b...e...d   bed

This drawing of a bed is helpful for new readers who confuse b with d

yes   yes   yes..

Coach read the word *lots* first, then new reader.
New reader read the rest of the words by themselves.
If your new reader hesitates or says a word incorrectly, wait 4 seconds....
Then you say the word correctly. Underline problem words and practise them again later.

lots ✓ ✓

bats

rams

hens

tins

zips

logs

dogs

pots

ten cats

six pigs

big hugs..

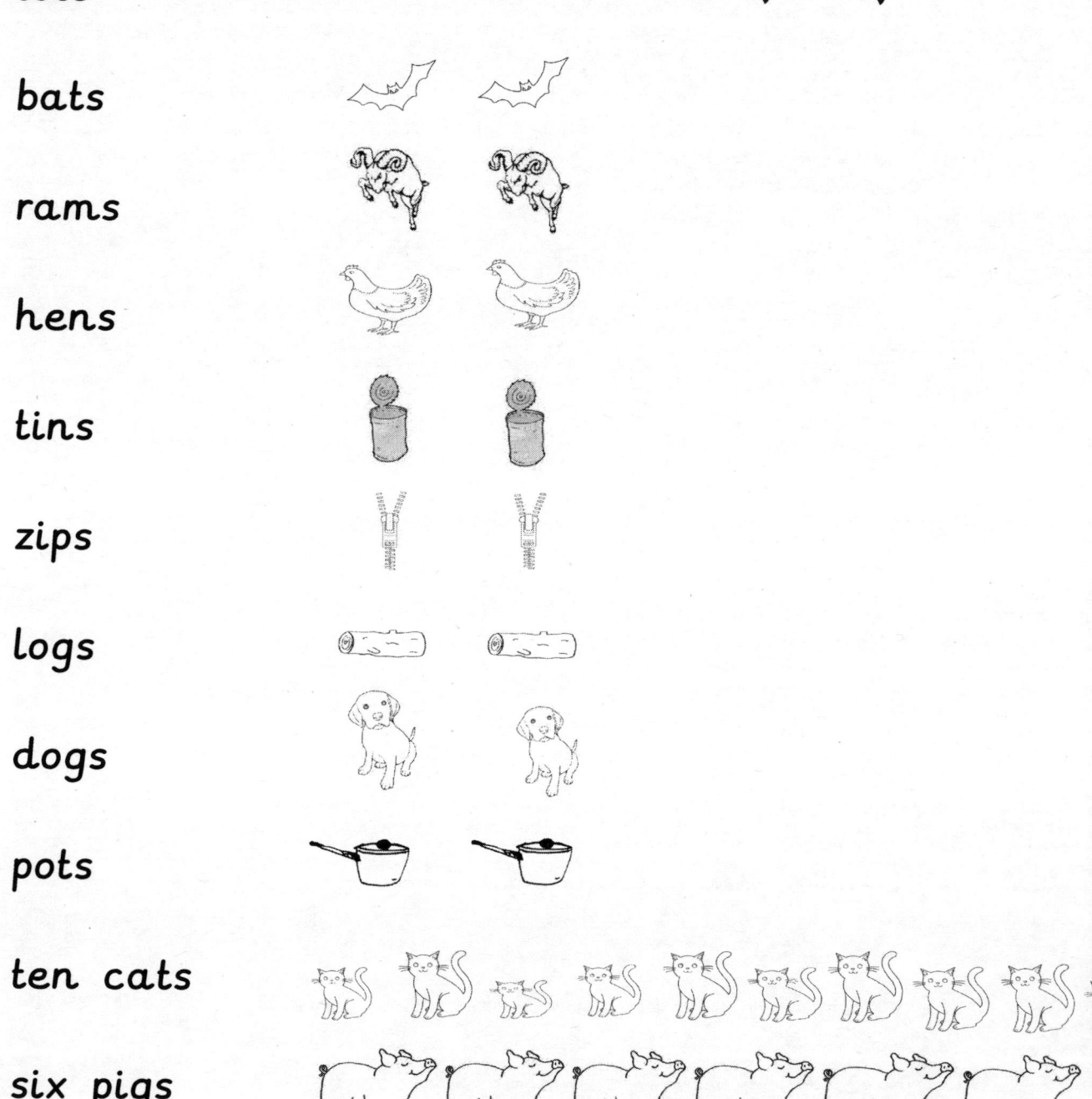

Coach read the words **the can ... the cans** first, then new reader.
New reader read the rest of the words by themselves.
If your new reader hesitates or says a word incorrectly, wait 4 seconds.....
Then <u>you</u> say the word correctly. Underline problem words and practise them again later.

✓ ✓

the can	the cans
the log	the logs
the dog	the dogs
the fin	the fins
the gun	the guns
the jet	the jets
the bat	the bats
the lip	the lips
the mug	the mugs
the jug	the jugs

tip top..

Coach ask your new reader to read the sentences.
(There may be no need for you to read first on this page)
If your new reader hesitates or says a word incorrectly, wait 4 seconds....
Then you say the word correctly. Underline problem words and practise them again later.

✓   ✓

the cat sat on the mat

the dog sat on the cat

the pig sat on the dog

the rat sat on the pig

the bug sat on the rat

the ants sat on the bug

the ants bit the bug

the bug bit the rat

the rat bit the pig

the pig bit the dog

the dog bit the cat

Yes................................ has got it.

Coach point and read : *this pig is wet.*
Then new reader read it + the following sentences.
If your new reader hesitates or says a word incorrectly, wait 4 seconds....
Then <u>you</u> say the word correctly. Underline problem words and practise them again later.
Don't forget *Say as you copy* for problem letters and words.

✓ ✓

this pig is wet

this pig is in the mud

this pig is in the wet mud

Coach point and read : *that is a man.*
Then new reader read it + the following sentences.

that is a man

that is a big man

that man has a fat dog

Coach point and read : *the hen is thin.*
Then new reader read it + the following sentences.

the hen is thin

this hen is thin

that hen is not thin

Yes this is it ………………………………….that is it .

Coach ask your new reader to read the sentences.
(There may be no need for you to read first on this page)
If your new reader hesitates or says a word incorrectly, wait 4 seconds....
Then you say the word correctly. Underline problem words and practise them again later.
Don't forget *Say as you copy* for problem letters and words.

✓   ✓

this man has ten cats

the cats sat on this bed

this bed had ten cats on it

this bed has a pup on it

the pup is thin

this pup is not a big dog

that dog bit the hens

that hen is a thin hen

that thin hen has an egg

that egg is not a big egg

Yes ………………………………………… that is a hit.

Big Letter-sounds

Coach point under each small and then big letter-sound and new reader read : a is A   etc.
(Please don't say ay bee cee dee...) Tick correct letters.
If your new reader hesitates or says a big letter-sound incorrectly, wait 4 seconds....
and then say it correctly. Underline problem big letter-sounds and practise them again later.

✓ ✓   ✓ ✓   ✓ ✓   ✓ ✓

a is A   b is B   c is C

d is D   e is E   f is F   g is G

h is H   i is I   j is J   k is K

l is L   m is M   n is N   o is O

p is P   q is Q   r is R   s is S

t is T   u is U   v is V   w is W

x is X   y is Y   z is Z

That is hot ....

Coach ask your new reader to read the sentences.
If your new reader hesitates or says a word incorrectly, wait 4 seconds....
and then say the word correctly. Underline problem words and practise them again later.
Don't forget *Say as you copy* for problem letters and words.

✓   ✓

Tom Cat met Sam Man.
Sam Man met Lox Ox.
Lox Ox met Vix Fox.
Vix Fox met Nat Bat.
Nat Bat met Egg Ant.
Egg Ant met Zog Dog.
Zog Dog met Jen Hen.
Jen Hen met Ig Pig.
Ig Pig met Guts Rat.
Guts Rat met Wiz Kid.
Wiz Kid met Up Up Pup.
Up Up Pup met Yak Yak Yak.

Yak Yak Yak the yak yaks : That is hot..................

Coach point and read : **The ship is big.**
Then new reader read it + the next sentences.
If your new reader hesitates or says a word incorrectly, wait 4 seconds....
and then say the word correctly. Underline problem words and practise them again later.
Don't forget *Say as you copy* for problem letters and words.

The ship is big.

Yes the ship is big.

The shop is shut.

Yes the shop is shut.

Coach point and read : **The ship has fish.**

Then new reader read it + the next sentences.

The ship has fish.

Yes the ship has fish.

The fish is in the dish.

Yes the fish is in the dish.

| Gosh, ... can read. |

Coach point and read : *Jack has a duck.*
Then new reader read it + the next sentences.
If your new reader hesitates or says a word incorrectly, wait 4 seconds....
and then say the word correctly.
Underline problem words and practise them again later.
Don't forget *Say as you copy* for problem words.

✓ ✓

Jack has a duck.

The duck is in his sack.

Jack has a duck in his sack.

The dog will lick.

The dog will lick his neck.

His neck is wet.

The back of his neck is wet.

Jack has lots of luck.

Yes Jack has lots of luck.

Jack will pick up the stick.

The stick is stuck in the mud.

Tick, tick, tick ....That has stuck.

Coach: Remind your new reader that letter-sound q is followed by a silent u (not queue or you!)
Point and read : Quick kiss quick kiss.
Then new reader read it + the next sentences.
If your new reader hesitates or says a word incorrectly, wait 4 seconds....and then say the word correctly.
Underline problem words and practise them again later.

> Tell your new reader how to pronounce the big letter I on its own.

Don't forget *Say as you copy* for problem letters and words.   ✓   ✓

Quick kiss quick kiss.

Quick kiss quick kiss.

The duck went quack quack quack.

Yes the duck went quack quack quack.

Quick quick quick I must run.

Quick quick quick I must run.

Quick quick quick I must quit.

I must quit.

Yes I must quit.

> That is quick ....

Coach point and read: *Tom has a big chin.*
Then new reader read it + the next sentences.
If your new reader hesitates or says a word incorrectly, wait 4 seconds and then say the word correctly.
Underline problem words and practise them again later.

Don't forget *Say as you copy* for problem letters and words.

✓   ✓

Tom has a big chin.

Yes Tom has a big chin.

Has Tom got a big chin ?

Yes Tom has got a big chin.

Is the dad a rich man ?

Yes the dad is a rich man.

Is Bob such a bad man ?

Bob is not such a bad man.

No Bob is not such a bad man.

Chin up......................can read such a lot.

Coach point and read : *Has the hen got a chick ?*
Then new reader read it + the next sentences.
If your new reader hesitates or says a word incorrectly, wait 4 seconds....
and then say the word correctly. Underline problem words and practise them again later.
Don't forget *Say as you copy* for problem letters and words.

✓ ✓

Has the hen got a chick ?

Yes the hen has got a chick.

This hen has got six chicks.

Cluck cluck cluck cluck cluck cluck.

Coach point and read : *Catch the chick.*
Then new reader read it + the next sentences.

Catch the chick.

Yes catch the chick.

Catch the six chicks.

Yes catch the six chicks.

Cluck cluck cluck cluck cluck cluck.

Tick tick tick ....

Coach point and read: c...l...a...p clap clap clap
Then new reader read it + the next sentences.
If your new reader hesitates or says a word incorrectly, wait 4 seconds and then say the word correctly.
Underline problem words and practise them again later.
Don't forget *Say as you copy* for problem letters and words.

c...l...a...p clap clap clap

✓ ✓ ✓ ✓ ✓ ✓

spot	spit	spat
frog	glad	drag
drop	blob	crab
swim	twin	jump
drum	plum	kept

New reader read 5-letter words:

stand	grand	swift
track	brick	frank
think	stamp	drink

New reader read 6-letter words:

splish	splash	splosh
strong	string	strung
shrink	shrimp	stench

clap clap ....fan...tas...tic = fantastic.

18

New reader read long words.

✓ ✓

fan...tas...tic = fantastic

con...ten...ted = contented

con...fi...dent = confident

stand...ing = standing

sing...ing = singing

dis...gus...ted = disgusted

re...mem...ber = remember

Sep...tem...ber = September

No...vem...ber = November

in...te...rest = interest

im...por...tant = important

un...der...pants = underpants

splen...did = splendid

fantastic, splendid...

Coco the chimp

Coach:

Read the whole of each new page of Coco the chimp out loud to your new learner <u>first.</u>

Then your new reader can read the page back to you as often as necessary.

Only move on to the next page if your reader is confident.

As before:

If your reader hesitates or says a word incorrectly,
wait 4 seconds.... before you say the word correctly.

Underline problem words and practise them again later.

Remember to use *Say as you copy*
for your new reader's problem words.

Coco the chimp

The sun is big.

The sun is big big big.

The sun is red.

The sun is red red red.

The sun is hot.

The sun is hot hot hot.

Coco the chimp is hot.

Coco the chimp is hot hot hot.

Yes yes yes ………………………………….can read.

Coach: only move on to the next page If your reader is confident.

page one

Coco the chimp is hot hot hot.

The moon is cool.

The moon is cool cool cool.

That is good.

That is good good good,

says Coco the chimp.

Good…………………………..can read well.

Coach: only move on to the next page If your reader is confident.

page two

I shall go to the moon.

I shall go go go to the moon,

says Coco the chimp.

I wish wish wish,

to go to the moon,

says Coco the chimp.

Good..................................**Go go go.**

Coach: only move on to the next page If your reader is confident.

page three

Quack quack quack,

says Luck Luck the duck.

Quack quack quack,

says Luck Luck the duck.

Quick quick quick,

says Luck Luck the duck.

Quick quick quick,

catch the moon with this stick,

says Luck Luck the duck.

Catch the moon with this stick.

Good, that is quick..

Coach: only move on to the next page If your reader is confident.

Pants the ant says,

pant, pant, pant,

pant, pant, pant.

Quick, quick, quick,

quick, quick, quick,

Too much to do,

too much to do.

Much too soon,

much too soon,

to go to the moon.

Shoo, shoo, shoo.

| Spot on.. Good, good, good. |

Coach: only move on to the next page If your reader is confident.

Hee hee hee,

hee hee hee,

says Shee Shee the sheep.

See that tree.

See that green tree.

The moon seems to be

on that green tree.

Hee hee hee,

hee hee hee,

says Shee Shee the sheep.

We can see that………………………………………….can read well.

Coach: only move on to the next page If your reader is confident.

Coco the chimp says,

when when when

will I go to the moon?

What what what

is the way to go

to the moon?

Where where where

is the way to go

to the moon?

Good…………………………… can read well.

Coach: only move on to the next page If your reader is confident.

Zoopy Loopy the bird sings his song.

> I loop the loop.
>
> I swoop and swoop.
>
> I loop the loop.
>
> I swoop and swoop.
>
> I loop the loop.
>
> I swoop and swoop.

Good, good, good...................................

Coach: only move on to the next page If your reader is confident.

Zoopy says,

see that boat.

See that boat.

See that green boat.

See that big green boat.

Get in the big green boat.

Get in the boat,

and then you can float.

Then you can float to the moon.

Boast that……….........................can read well.

Coach: only move on to the next page If your reader is confident.

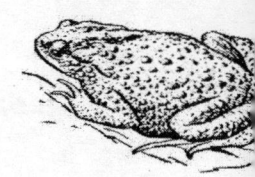

Croaky the toad sings his song.

> I am a toad,
>
> a big bad toad.
>
> Croak croak croak.
>
> I am a toad,
>
> a big bad toad.
>
> Croak croak croak.

A toast for..

Coach: only move on to the next page If your reader is confident.

Croaky says,

see that road over there.

See that long black road over there.

Coco says,

where where where ?

Croaky says,

that long black road over there.

That is the road to the moon.

Yes, that is the road to the moon.

Coco says,

where where where ?

Good……………………is on the road.

Coach: only move on to the next page If your reader is confident.

page eleven

Browny Brown the owl sings his song.

> Who are you?
>
> Who are you?
>
> Who are you?
>
> Who who who?
>
> Who are you?
>
> Who are you?
>
> Who are you?
>
> Who who who?

Now……………..can read well.

Coach: only move on to the next page If your reader is confident.

page twelve

Who am I?

I am Coco the chimp, says Coco.

How how how can I get to the moon?

Do not go now,

says Browny Brown,

with a frown.

Not now, not now, not now, not now.

Just let the sun go down,

says Browny Brown,

with a frown.

Now that is tiptop……………… How hot is that now?

Coach: only move on to the next page If your reader is confident.

Mouse sings his song.

> Out out out shouts the man.
>
> Out out out shouts the girl.
>
> Out out out shouts the boy.
>
> In in in shouts the mouse.
>
> In in in shouts the mouse.

Shout it out. We are proud of ....

Coach: only move on to the next page If your reader is confident.

page fourteen

Coco says,

Mouse, my old pal Mouse,

I want to go to the moon.

What about me, says Mouse ?

What about me, says Mouse ?

I want to go back in the house.

Yes, I want to go back in the house.

Shout it out………………….................reads well.
Out…stand…ing = outstanding. Yes, outstanding.

Coach: only move on to the next page If your reader is confident.

Go Go the gorilla sings his song.

> I spy with my
> big brown eye
> a teeny weeny
> little fly.
> I spy with my
> big brown eye
> a teeny weeny
> little fly

Good……………………….will fly.

Coach: only move on to the next page If your reader is confident.

page sixteen

Hang on, hang on,

says Go Go the gorilla.

That is not a fly in the sky.

No, no, that is not a fly in the sky.

That is Coco the chimp I can spy.

Yup, that is Coco the chimp I can spy.

Coco says,

I try and I try and I try

to get to the moon.

I do try and try to get to the moon.

Yes I do try.

Can you help ?

...................................can fly now.

Go Go the gorilla says to Coco,

Keep your feet on the ground.

Stop jumping around.

Keep your feet on the ground.

Stop messing around.

Keep your feet on the ground.

Stop fooling around.

Keep your feet on the ground.

Stop mucking around.

Keep your feet on the ground.

Better and better…………………outstanding, outstanding.

Coach: only move on to the next page If your reader is confident.

Queen Queeny the queen bee sings.

> Buzz, buzz, buzz,
> I am buzzing
> around my hive.
> Buzz, buzz, buzz,
> I am humming
> around my hive.
> Buzz, buzz, buzz,
> I am singing
> around my hive.
> Buzz, buzz, buzz,
> I am flying
> around my hive.

………………………..is flying.

Coach: only move on to the next page If your reader is confident.

Queen Queeny says,

so why are you here, Coco?

Why are you here, Coco,

and what do you want?

Coco says,

I am trying to get to the moon.

That is what I am trying to do.

That is what I keep on trying

and trying and trying to do.

..................................is flying along now.

Coach: only move on to the next page If your reader is confident.

Queen Queeny says, you may sit down here.

She says, you may sit down here, Coco.

Queen Queeny says, stay stay stay

and play all day.

She says, stay stay stay and play all day.

You may just stay here and play all day.

Just stay here and play all day, Coco.

That is what I say.

What a star……………………….........................**is !**

Coach: only move on to the next page If your reader is confident.

Beano the rat sings his song.

I eat this bean.

I eat that bean.

I eat beans, beans, beans.

I eat big beans.

I eat small beans.

I eat beans, beans, beans.

I eat brown beans.

I eat green beans.

I eat beans, beans, beans.

We mean to say....................... is a star new reader.

Coach: only move on to the next page If your reader is confident.

Coco says,

tell me how to reach the moon, Beano.

Teach me how to reach the moon, Beano.

I can teach you how to reach the moon.

Yes indeed, I can teach you how to reach the moon, says Beano.

Each rat will stand on top of the next rat.

Yes, each rat will stand on top of the next rat.

That is how each of us rats will get there.

Yes indeed, that is how each of us rats will get there.

....is a very good new reader, and has a very good teacher.

Coach: only move on to the next page If your reader is confident.

Little Dung Dung the beetle sings her song.

> I am a little beetle,
> short and fat.
> I roll dung
> and that is that.
> I am a little beetle,
> black and wide.
> I roll dung
> to the other side.
> I am a little beetle
> and I smell.
> I roll dung
> and you can tell.

Fantastic, fantastic ……………………………………

Coach: only move on to the next page If your reader is confident.

Hello Little Dung Dung, says Coco.
Can you or your beetle pals help me?
I am trying to get to the moon.

Go along the middle of the jungle.
Along the middle of the jungle is the way,
says Little Dung Dung, the beetle.
The middle of the jungle is the way we beetles go.

Later on Coco said,
I will not go along the middle of the jungle.
No, I will not go along the middle of the jungle.
The moon is in the sky.
It is not in the middle of the jungle.

Fantastic, and that is no joke………………………….

Coach: only move on to the next page If your reader is confident.

Ruff Ruff the dog sings his song.

> I like a bone.
> Yes, yes I do.
> I like a bone.
> Just give it here.
> I love a bone.
> Just give it here.
> I need a bone,
> Just give it here.
> I want a bone,
> Just give it here.

We love your progress……………..........It is outstanding.

Coach: only move on to the next page If your reader is confident.

Coco says to Ruff Ruff,

could you help me to go to the moon?

Ruff Ruff licks his paw and says,

have you got a bone for me?

Could you give me a little bone?

Could you?

Would you give me a little bone?

Would you?

I can see you have no bone for me.

Ruff Ruff moans and groans.

Outstanding progress..................................

Coach: only move on to the next page If your reader is confident.

Well listen to me, Coco,

says Ruff Ruff.

I could howl at the moon,

yup, yup, yup.

You could howl at the moon,

yup, yup, yup.

We could howl at the moon,

yup, yup, yup.

We could all howl at the moon,

yup, yup, yup.

That would be much more fun.

That would be so much more fun.

Yup, yup, yup.

..................................should have a big clap.

Coach: only move on to the next page If your reader is confident.

I did not like to mention it,

said Coco much later on.

No, I did not like to mention it.

I do not think that could work.

I do not think that would work at all.

Howling would not do much good at all.

No, howling would not do much good at all.

....should have a big, big clap.

Coach: only move on to the next page If your reader is confident.

page twenty-nine

Oily Coily the snake sings his song.

> I love sliding in the sand.
> I like spitting on your hand.
> I have poison in my bite.
> I can spit at you with spite.
> What makes me sad ?
> They say I'm bad.
>
> I love chewing on some bugs.
> I like giving them some hugs.
> I make noises in your face.
> I think spoiling fun is ace.
> What makes me sad ?
> They say I'm bad.

....is making outstanding progress.

Coach: only move on to the next page If your reader is confident.

Oily Coily the snake hisses,

what is that loud noise ?

Is that you making that loud noise, Coco,

you noisy, noisy, noisy chimp ?

Sorry about that, says Coco.

Do you know the way to the moon ?

Yes, yes, yes, I know the way.

Yes, yes, yes, I know the way.

But I will never ever say.

Now off you go, you noisy, noisy chimp.

..............................knows the way to read well.

Coach: only move on to the next page If your reader is confident.

I don't like to mention it,

said Coco much later on.

No, I don't like to mention it.

But I don't think Oily Coily knows the way.

I don't think he knows at all.

I don't think he does.

> ....knows how to read very well, for sure.

Coach: only move on to the next page If your reader is confident.

Brains the hippo sings his song.

> Brains is my name.
> Yes Brains is my name,
> and I wait and I wait,
> and I wait for rain.
> Yes I wait and I wait,
> and I wait for rain.

Hello Brains, says Coco.

It looks like it will rain today.

I hope so, I hope so, says Brains.

My water hole needs rain.

Yes, my water hole needs rain.

Let's hope for rain.

It should rain today.

Splendid reading..........................**That is the main thing, for sure.**

Coach: only move on to the next page If your reader is confident.

I hate to bother you.
Yes, I hate to bother you.
I hate to be a pain.
I hate to mention it,
says Coco.
But do you know the way
to the moon, Brains?

Yawn, yawn, yawn, says Brains.
Yawn, yawn, yawn.

Coco points at the moon in the sky.
I am trying to get there.

Yawn, yawn, yawn, says Brains.
Yawn, yawn, yawn.

Fantastic, splendid!

What a good new reader……………………........is!

Coach: only move on to the next page If your reader is confident.

Yawn, yawn, yawn, says Brains.
Look in the water hole.
What do you see?
I see water, says Coco.
The water is green and brown
and black and blue.
Yes, the water is green and brown
and black and blue.

Yawn, yawn, yawn, says Brains.
See that white ball.
See that big, white ball in the water.
That big, white ball is the moon.

.................................is a very good new reader, and that is true.

Coach: only move on to the next page If your reader is confident.

I don't like to mention it,
said Coco later on.
I don't think that Brains lives up
to his name.
That white ball was not the moon.
That white ball in the water hole
was not the moon.
That white ball in the water hole
was the reflection of the moon.
Yes, that white ball was the reflection
of the moon in the water hole.

> **Excellent. We must mention that ………………........... can read long words like fantastic and reflection and excellent. And that is true.**

Coach: only move on to the next page If your reader is confident.

Worry Worries the ostrich bird sings.

> My name is Worry Worries.
> I have problem, problem, problems.
> I have worry, worry, worries.
> I have trouble, trouble, troubles.
> I have worry worry worries.
> I have danger, danger, dangers.
> I have worry, worry, worries.
> So my head goes in the sand.
> Yes my head goes in the sand.

Excellent, excellent……………………………………………
too true, too true, too true.

Coach: only move on to the next page If your reader is confident.

When Worry Worries the ostrich bird
sees Coco coming along the road,
her head goes in the sand.
Yes, her head goes in the sand.

Later on Coco said,
I hate to mention it,
but that was a waste of my time.
That was a real waste of my time.
Worry Worries buries her head in the sand.
She just buries her head in the sand.
She always buries her head in the sand
when we need her help.
What a waste of my time !

Excellent...................no worries there, no worries there at all.

Coach: only move on to the next page If your reader is confident.

Gee-gee the gentle giraffe sings his song.

> We giraffes are gentle.
> And we giraffes are tall.
> We giraffes are certainly,
> most certainly not small.
> We giraffes are gentle.
> And we giraffes are nice.
> We giraffes are certainly,
> most certainly not mice.

....is certainly, most certainly, a good reader.

Coach: only move on to the next page If your reader is confident.

Hello Coco, you cute little chimp,

says Gee-gee the gentle giraffe.

You could stand on my head.

Yes you could.

You could stand on my head.

Yes you could, says Gee-gee the gentle giraffe.

But I would stay down instead.

I would stay where you are.

The moon is far too far.

Yes the moon is far too far,

says Gee-gee the gentle giraffe.

Very nice, in fact excellent………………………………
Excellent, excellent, excellent.

Coach: only move on to the next page If your reader is confident.

I don't like to mention it,

said Coco later on.

No, I don't like to mention it.

But I am sure that Gee-gee, that nice, gentle giraffe does not know the way to the moon.

I am sure that Gee-gee that nice, gentle giraffe does not know the way to the moon

In fact no-one seems to know the way.

It is time to see Big Chief Jelly Belly.

Excellent. We like to write that...................is a great new reader.

Coach: only move on to the next page If your reader is confident.

Yes, it is time to see Big Chief Jelly Belly.

I had better take him a banana.

He likes a bit of fruit,

and he loves bananas.

It is his birthday today.

So I will sing to him.

But I had better practise first.

Yes, I had better practise first.

Happy birthday to you,

happy birthday to you,

happy birthday,

dear Big Chief Jelly Belly,

happy birthday to you.

Excellent ……………………….is a great new reader.

Coach: only move on to the next page If your reader is confident.

Big Chief Jelly Belly the elephant sings his song.

> Come to the water hole.
>
> It is night.
>
> Come to the water hole.
>
> That is right.
>
> Come to the water hole.
>
> Moon is bright.
>
> Come to the water hole.
>
> Have some light.
>
> Come to the water hole.
>
> What a sight !

Excellent, outstanding……………………is a great new reader, and that is right. Yes indeed, that is right.

Coach: only move on to the next page If your reader is confident.

Coco comes through the bush,

through the village,

through the jungle,

and through the trees.

Big Chief Jelly Belly the elephant is dancing.

I love singing.

I love dancing.

One two three four five,

one two three four five,

quick quick slow slow quick,

quick quick slow slow quick,

one two three four five,

one two three four five.

Right my boy, says Big Chief Jelly Belly,

sing happy birthday to me.

Then you can give me that banana.

Give me that fruit, my boy.

 I love a bit of fruit.

I love nice and juicy fruit.

Yes, nice and juicy fruit, is what I like.

Then we will get this moon stuff sorted out once and for all.

Yes, we will get this moon matter sorted out once and for all.

Yes, we will get this moon business sorted out once and for all.

Excellent……………………….super star!

Coach: only move on to the next page If your reader is confident.

When I was your age, my boy,

just a little elephant of seven or eight,

I had a dream about going to the moon.

But remember this, my boy, just remember this,

remember to keep your dreams.

The moon will always be here,

and your friends will always be near.

Yes, the moon will always be here,

and your friends will always be near.

That is my message, says Big Chief Jelly Belly, the elephant.

The end.

Congratulations to you both.
Keep on reading and writing...

page forty-five

Your song:

Each one teach a friend to read.

> Each one teach a friend to read.
> Yes, yes, yes, we'll plant that seed.
>
> Each one teach a friend to write.
> Yes, yes, yes, we'll fly that kite.
>
> Each one teach a friend to count.
> Yes, yes, yes, it's that amount.
>
> Each one teach a friend to build.
> Yes, yes, yes, our lives fulfilled.
>
> Each one teach a friend to grow.
> Yes, yes, yes, so then we'll know.

Small Letter Writing Practice

a a a

b b b

c c c

d d d

e e e

f f f

g g g

h h h

i i i

j j j

k k k

l l l

m m m

n n n

o o o

p p p

q q q

r r r

s s s

t t t

u u u

v v v

w w w

x x x

y y y

z z z

Big Letter Writing Practice

a = A A A ....

b = B B B ....

c = C C C ....

d = D D D ....

e = E E E ....

f = F F F ....

g = G G G ....

h = H H H ....

i=I I I
j=J J J
k=K K K
l=L L L
m=M M M
n=N N N
o=O O O
p=P P P
q=Q Q Q

r=R R R

s=S S S

t=T T T

u=U U U

v=V V V

w=W W W

x=X X X

y=Y Y Y

z=Z Z Z